Blind Faith

WALKING BY FAITH TO RECEIVE WHAT YOU CANNOT SEE

ROBERT R. THIBODEAU

Robert Thibodeau

BLIND FAITH
Walking by Faith To Receive What You Cannot See

Robert R Thibodeau

Robert Thibodeau

Copyright © 2015 Robert R Thibodeau

All rights reserved.

ISBN: 0692403930
ISBN-13: 978-0692403938

All Scripture is taken from the Authorized King James Version Red Letter Edition Bible. In some instances, at the discretion of the author, modern word usage is used to make the scripture clearer. In these instances, the context of the scripture was not changed.

Blind Faith: Walking by Faith to Receive What You Cannot See

I must say my friend, Robert Thibodeau did a great job writing this book. **Blind Faith** is an excellent tool for building faith in every believer's heart. Not only does the book help the reader understand what *faith* is truly all about, but the author gives the historical background and traditions in many settings and situations. This creates a better understanding of the full picture of what Jesus was talking about, so that faith is taught more clearly. I especially enjoyed the challenge of the 'Selah' at the end of each chapter, encouraging us to 'pause and think about that'. As we are doers of the word, and not hearers only, **Blind Faith** encourages us to truly be '*walking by faith to receive what we cannot see!*'

Dove Morgan,
Loving Hearts Ministry
Crossroads Ranch Ministries
Bristow, Oklahoma

In today's world where trials and tribulations seem to grow daily and where a Believer's Faith needs to be finely-tuned and working properly to overcome worldly obstacles, Robert Thibodeau's new book, "Blind Faith – Walking By Faith To Receive What You Cannot See" spiritually hits the mark. The book provides solid foundational Biblical teaching that will help keep a Believer's faith strong, developing your Kingdom witness to the world, and will help to produce abundant fruit in your life. "Blind Faith" will help you develop 'eyes that see', what the Lord has prepared for you from the foundation of the world!

Dr Will Pantin
President and Apostolic leader
Great Joy in the City Ministries
Bond Servants of Christ Ministerial Fellowship

Robert Thibodeau

DEDICATION

This book is dedicated to my grandson (and life long golf partner), Christopher. As this book goes to press, he will be turning 18 years old and heading out into this world on his own. It is my prayer, that the insights, examples, teachings and many discussions we have had (mainly during the many hours we spent together on the golf course since he was age 4) will inspire him and bring to remembrance that Faith in God should always be the number one priority in a persons life.

I may not have always done the right thing, but God was Faithful and Just to His Word…and when I repented of the things I did wrong, He forgave me because of the Blood of Jesus. You need to remember that, for when you mess up (and you will) – Jesus is right there to help…if you ask Him.

You have been my "pride and joy" ever since the day you were born…it is hard for me to believe that now I, your grandmother and your parents – must "turn you loose" into this world. I know that you will be successful at whatever the Lord has planned for you to do with your life. Just remember, you must "seek first His Kingdom and His Righteousness, then – ALL these other things will be added to you." (Matthew 6:33).

When I am no longer here on this earth, I know that there will be a day when we will be together again…and we will play the longest par 5 in all of creation! There will be no "hooks" or "slices" and every shot will be perfect – right down the middle!

I love you Christopher, never forget that…

PAPA

Robert Thibodeau

Blind Faith: Walking by Faith to Receive What You Cannot See

CONTENTS

1	Chapter One	Pg 11
2	Chapter Two	Pg 19
3	Chapter Three	Pg 23
4	Chapter Four	Pg 31
5	Chapter Five	Pg 41
6	Chapter Six	Pg 53
7	Chapter Seven	Pg 59
8	Chapter Eight	Pg 65
9	Chapter Nine	Pg 71
10	Chapter Ten	Pg 81
11	Chapter Eleven	Pg 89
12	Chapter Twelve	Pg 97
13	Chapter Thirteen	Pg 105
	Prayer of Salvation	Pg 117
	About the Author	Pg 119

Robert Thibodeau

CHAPTER ONE

"And as Jesus passed by, He saw a man which was blind from his birth." **John 9:1**

One day, Jesus was walking through Jerusalem. Some scholars say this particular area described, in John 9:1, was just outside the city gates. They don't know if Jesus was just leaving or if He was just entering, but He was just outside the gates of the city. The setting is near an area called the pool of Siloam. It was a busy area and there were a lot of people passing by daily. There was a blind man there, who had been born blind. He was there trying to receive enough in alms, or offerings, from the people that walked by, so he could buy something to eat.

There were two pools located there, which were separated in distance by about half a mile or maybe even up to three quarters of a mile (depending on which Bible scholar you are referencing). One pool was the pool of Siloam and the other was the pool of Solomon and they were located on opposite ends of the Temple complex area. These pools were areas where the people had to be "ceremonially cleansed" before entering the Temple area. The custom in that day was to have the people be cleansed before they could enter the temple area to worship. It was, basically, a ceremonial bath.

A person would step down into the pool, walk across and then climb back up the steps on the other side. It could be likened to what the baptismal pools are in some churches today. Some baptismal pools are set up where a person enters from one side, steps down into the pool, gets immersed and then walks back up the other side. These were ceremonial areas, not "bath houses," but in order to enter the Temple complex a person had to be ceremonially cleansed. These pools served as the ceremonial cleansing spots.

On this particular day, as described in John chapter 9, there was a blind man there, begging for alms as the people entered or left the city of Jerusalem. He was an adult who had to be led around. He was blind so he could not walk around town by himself. More than likely, he would have had someone lead him by the hand around town. There were a lot of people walking around Jerusalem and it would be virtually impossible for this person to walk around without help. There were animals walking around and there was a lot of people walking around; there were merchants putting carts out by their stores and shops and they were stacking their merchandise for sale... so a blind man would have to have had someone lead him around everywhere he went.

If you've never been in a blind person's house, let me just explain it to you... It is usually one of the most organized, clean and kept places that you could ever imagine. The old adage, "There is a place for everything and everything in its place," is true for a blind person because they have memorized every square foot of that house. They know where every lamp table is located and where every chair and every foot-stool is situated. The blind person needs to know where everything is - because they can't see!

So if you come over to visit and they ask:

"Would you like a drink of water? Or some tea?" or something similar. If you said "Sure I'll get it, you just stay there and I'll take care of it," they would probably say, "No, no, I'll get it".

They're not doing that completely out of politeness, but mostly out of necessity. If you were to get your own water or tea, you might put the glass down somewhere and they would not be able to find it. Or you may put the teapot down somewhere where they would not be able to easily find it. If you were to leave a dirty dish on the counter, they may knock it over and break it while searching for it. So when they insist on serving you, they really are doing this because they need to know exactly where everything is.

Outside of the house, the blind person needs help in negotiating their way around unfamiliar settings. In Jesus day, there were ox carts as well as vegetable carts and merchants stacking things to sell and people walking around. Therefore, they would have needed someone to help them get from point A to point B.

Blind Faith: Walking by Faith to Receive What You Cannot See

This blind guy obviously had someone take him to this area each morning to ask alms. His contribution to the family was to ask alms from people as they went in or out of the city. He probably did not earn much, but what he did earn helped the family take care of him. They would then come back later in the day and escort him back home.

This particular day, as Jesus and the Disciples were walking by, they saw this man sitting there. The disciples asked, *"Master, who did sin, this man or his parents, that he was born blind?"* They were probably close enough to this blind man where he might have heard them talking. It is well documented that blind people actually develop their other senses to make up for their absence of sight. So this blind man could hear almost any conversation taking place that was near him. He most likely heard the disciples and Jesus talking about him and discussing the reason he had been born blind.

Notice also, both the disciples and Jesus knew about this man's condition. They knew the history behind it. They knew he had been born blind. They were familiar with him asking for alms each and every day.

This man had heard all of the reasons before, such as, "either he had sinned in his previous life or while in the womb of his mother" (although nobody could ever explain 'how' he would have sinned in his mothers' womb); how his parents had committed some terrible sin and now he was "paying for it" to punish them (how him being blind would punish his parents, nobody could explain adequately, either); How God was trying to "teach" him something through this blindness (but nobody could ever explain what that "something" was)... and on and on it would go.

So, as he started to listen to this group of men approach him – he would have heard them call Jesus "Master," and it would have gotten his attention (although in that cultural area, "Master" was often used as like "boss" today - so he would not have immediately recognized them as addressing the question to Jesus).

Selah: What afflictions have you had to endure in your life? It could be some physical ailment or financial problem. It could be relationship problems or family problems. It could be any number of things where it seems like life has dealt you a pretty bad hand.

I have "Good News" for you today! Jesus is aware of your situation! He knows all about you and what you are going through. As we continue along in this study, you will see some things this blind man realized – and the end result was his healing.

Stick with the study…and Jesus will do the same for you!

Robert Thibodeau

Chapter Two

Let's read the scripture in John chapter 9:1-4...

"And as Jesus passed by he saw a man who was blind from birth and his disciples said 'Master who had sinned, this man or his parents that he was born blind?' and Jesus answered, 'Neither has this man sinned nor his parents but that the word of God should be manifested in him. I must work the works of him who sent me, while it is day, for the night is coming when no man can work.'"

It was a common belief of the Jews that parents, who were sinful or amiss in their obedience to God or their religious duties, could pass the result of their sins on to their unborn children. Some held to the false view of pre-existence or reincarnation in which the child, in its previous life, had sinned and therefore caused the deformity in its present life.

And that gives us some insight into the religious views

of the Jews, which came from the teachings of the Pharisees. Although they were informed of the Law, they were clearly deficient in their understanding of the origins of sin.

Romans chapter 5 verse 12 states: *"Wherefore as by one man sin entered into the world, and death by sin; and so death passed upon all men, so that all have sinned."*

When Adam sinned as the forerunner of the human race, his sin passed to all men "the nature of sin." Every person after him that has been born into this earth, from Adam until now, has a carnal nature of sin.

The phrase, "to sin" basically means "to miss the mark." Jesus did not deal with these incorrect beliefs that the Disciples raised. It was not this man that had sinned nor was this a result of his parents sin.

In Romans chapter 7 verse 5, Paul said:

"For when we were in the flesh, the motions of sins, which were by the law, did work in our members to bring forth fruit unto death."

Here, the term "flesh" describes the carnal, wicked nature of man, which is the source of all incorrect doing and rebellion against God. A man (or woman), in this natural, "un-regenerated" state, can only do what their nature allows them to do.

Paul says in First Corinthians chapter 2 verse 14,

"The natural man receives not things of the spirit of God: for they are foolishness to him: neither can he know them because they are spiritually discerned."

The unbeliever, in our natural state, has no spiritual nature that reflects the Nature of God. This type of spiritual nature is only received by the Holy Spirit when a person believes in Jesus Christ as the way for salvation and is born again.

Let's look now at John chapter 9:5-7

"As long as I am in the world I am the light of the world."

Jesus used here a common expression in the Jewish culture that compared day and night to life and death. While it was day and light He was alive and able to achieve God's will. Right here, however, Jesus is forecasting His death and is referring to it as night - when a man cannot work because of the darkness:

"When he had hence spoken, he spat on the ground, and make clay of the spittle, and he anointed the eyes of the blind man with clay and said to him, 'go wash in the pool of Siloam, (Which is by interpretation, "Sent"). He went his way therefore, and washed, and came seeing."

Jesus actually states here that He was "light to the world" as long as He was in the world. The blind guy was in darkness and when he encountered Jesus, he came to the "Light of the world!"

Selah: Have you ever used the expression "I can't see a way out of this…"? Perhaps it is because you are trying to find your way out while stumbling in the dark. If you are relying on your natural abilities to fix spiritual problems, you will stumble every time.

Allow Jesus to be your guide. Turn to Him; turn your problem over to Him…and ask Him to lead you into the Light! For He is the True Light!

CHAPTER THREE

Luke explains why Jesus came into the world:

Luke chapter 1 verse 78 - 79

"Through the tender mercies of our God whereby the dayspring from on high has visited us, to give light to those who sit in darkness and in the shadow of death, to guide our feet in the way of peace."

Jesus then spoke once more to His disciples, stating *"I am the light of the world; he that follows me shall not walk in darkness but have the light of life."* **(John 8:12)**

Jesus is the light of the world and, as the light of the world, He was referring to the truth that He was the Messiah who came into the earth to free men from the curse of sin and of death. This Jesus was the Word, translated as "Logos" which means the Truth/reality - and here He is called "The Light." In John chapter 3 verse 19 you can also see this truth:

"And this is the condemnation, that light is come into the

world, and men loved darkness rather than light, because their deeds were evil."

Now, I want you to understand a couple of very important things about this story. Jesus' appeal in Judea and Jerusalem and among individuals was reaching its apex at this time. This blind man must have heard about Jesus. Everybody was talking about Jesus and how He would heal everybody who came to Him. We have already seen how this individual needed to have others help him walk around as it would have been almost impossible for him to walk around the city by himself.

We also understand he most likely had heard about Jesus and that he most likely heard how Jesus had already healed other blind and sick folks that came to him. He probably even knew blind Bartimaeus (or at least knew about him)! It is most likely that he has asked the people (probably his family members) who led him to the gates everyday (so he could ask for alms) to: "Take me to Jesus! Find this guy Jesus! I know he will heal me!"

And his relatives are probably like some other people you and I know today. Maybe you are associated with a healing ministry or some other faith work and people will state things like "No, that's not real - that's all phony! Those are individuals sent there; it was pre-planned; they're stooges attempting to get individuals to give offerings; it's not real! Do not believe all of those things, etc., etc." I know individuals like that and I am sure you do also. Many of them are in churches!

Well, the exact same thing was being stated in the days of Jesus as well.

The family members he had asked, as well as individuals who were leading him around, had most likely informed him: "We do not have time for that faith stuff. We do not have time to go and locate where this Jesus person is...and we do not have time to take you over there and then wait for him to heal you - or probably "not" heal you. Then, if he does not heal you, you're going to need us to bring you back home again. That means we would have squandered the whole day - because we just can't leave you there. We would have to wait there all day - and we have heard that Jesus guy can preach for hours!"

In other words - they don't truly believe him and they sure don't think Jesus can heal him, either. Otherwise, they would have already had him in amongst Jesus' meetings! So, he needed to try and navigate himself into a position where Jesus could "see him."

He understood Jesus was coming and going in and out of Jerusalem recently and that He had been teaching in the temple complex. So he would ask the people leading him around to "take me over there... let me sit over here today." Now, considering that he was blind, he couldn't sit around until Jesus came to town and then try to follow the crowd along to where Jesus was going to be preaching that day. He had to try and get into a position where Jesus would be able to "see him." Maybe, if he could do that, Jesus would have compassion on him and come over to where he was. It was his only hope.

I believe this man was praying for an encounter with Jesus.

Then, one day as he was listening to what was going on

around him, he heard a group of men stop near where he was sitting...

Then he heard the question: *"Master, why was he born blind?"* **(John 9:2)**

We have already discussed the natural concept taught in that day, how either his sin or his parents' sin caused him to be born blind. Then he hears Jesus say,

"He has not sinned nor has his parents sinned, b*ut that the works of God should be manifest in him."*

He had never heard that before! He had always been told he was just "in the way" or that "God could never use him" and things like that. But now, he has heard something that is completely new to him. He was probably pondering what that could mean when... somebody put something on his eyes!

Jesus had spit on the ground and made clay. The blind guy did not understand what was going on. He was just sitting there listening to the conversation and pondering what had been said when, all of a sudden, Jesus put this clay on his eyes! It most likely took him aback a bit

– he didn't understand what was going on! He may even have asked, "What are you doing?"

Which is when Jesus told him *"Go and wash in the pool of Siloam."*

And he most likely asked, "Why?" He also realized the pool of Siloam was a long way off – half way across town. He may have even said, "Solomon's pool is right around the corner. Why can't I go over there?"

And more than likely, one of Jesus' disciples leaned over and whispered in his ears, "Jesus has instructed you to go to the pool of Siloam - have faith and believe this..."

Which is when he must have recognized that it was Jesus - THE JESUS - who had actually done this to him. At this point, he had a choice to make... either to believe it and obey - or reject it and wonder, "If it would have worked."

That must have been magnificent in his ears to understand that Jesus was the one who had actually done this. Jesus had put "something" on his eyes, but he didn't know what it was! He didn't know it was spit and dirt!

Jesus already said this man had actually not sinned and neither had his mom or dad sinned! That implied he was still in covenant standing as a descendant of Abraham... That meant he did not need to not be blind! If that truly was the case...healing belonged to him!

In his spirit - he "understood" it was real! He simply had to trust and do exactly what Jesus stated. Jesus said *"go wash in the pool of Siloam."* So that is what he was going to do! Now, all he had to do was find someone who could lead him across town to the pool of Siloam...

SELAH: Sometimes, in order to achieve our breakthrough in the areas we are hurting in (physical, financial, social or spiritual), we are told to do something that makes absolutely no sense in the natural. Whoever heard, if you were in severe lack of financial resources, to "give money away to someone else in need?" The "natural man" believes he should "hold onto all I got!" But, the Bible clearly says,

"GIVE – and it shall be given unto you…a good measure, pressed down and shaken together – men running over shall give into your bosom." (Luke 6:38)

If you know you have heard from God – do what He has told you to do. Even if it does not make any sense in the natural, do what He tells you to do! God does not need your last $5 to bless you financially (for example). He is looking for "Faith in His Word!" He is seeing if you really, really trust Him. So, when you obey what He has told you to do – He then has FAITH to work with in your behalf.

CHAPTER FOUR

Let me attempt to clear something up. Some of you may be asking, "Why did Jesus need to put spit and clay on this man's eyes and tell him to go wash in the pool of Siloam? Why couldn't Jesus just put his hands on him and heal him like He did other people? Others had actually received their sight with Jesus simply laying hands on them, like blind Bartimaeus. Why couldn't Jesus simply do that for him, too?"

I prayed long and hard about this and asked the Lord about it.

The Lord revealed to me the reason WHY He could not simply lay hands on the blind man: **it's because of Faith**. Those who sought Jesus out, like blind Bartimaeus and others, came TO Jesus, utilizing their Faith and putting a demand on their Faith for Jesus to heal them.

Jesus requires Faith in order to affect the end result.

That's why in His hometown, in Matthew 13:58, Jesus could not heal many individuals due to the fact that they didn't have faith to believe. As a matter of fact, in Matthew 13:55, they believed he was just the "Carpenter's child who lived down the street."

If you do a careful Bible research study, you will certainly find that in every circumstance where Jesus came across individuals that did not seek Him out first, He required them to "do something" just to have a little bit of faith for Him to utilize and to achieve the desired result. In this case, healing this blind man and providing him his sight.

We can also look at the story about the widowed woman whose only son had actually passed away and was being carried out of town in a casket as Jesus came walking into town. In Luke 7:11-17, we can see how Jesus could do nothing unless the widow woman showed some Faith.

She is crying and there were many people with her and they were all crying and carrying on. It was popular in those days to hire "weepers" for funerals. The number of people that would be crying at your funeral calculated your status in life.

Because that was the tradition, those following the widow would be crying and carrying on also. The saying "misery loves company" was true in this situation. The people were crying and carrying on as if they were truly in mourning and grief stricken...which would just exasperate the poor old widow lady and keep her in a state of grief as well.

The Bible says, *"Jesus had compassion on her"* - most likely because He understood she now had no one to care for her. He may even have known this woman. He went up to her and said, *"Woman, don't weep!"* **(verse 13).**

Because that was the custom and the culture, this took "Faith" for her to stop crying! She had a reason to weep! Jesus simply states to her *"Do not weep!"* She probably recognized who Jesus was. She most likely reasoned within herself, "Stop weeping? Why? I have a reason to weep! But, if He says to 'stop weeping'- maybe He is going to do something to give me a reason to stop weeping! YES! That could be it!" She musters up all the Faith she has - and stops weeping in order to see exactly what Jesus is going to do!

When she stopped crying, she had accomplished what Jesus had told her to do. That was enough Faith for Jesus to work with. When she "obeyed His Word" – she showed Faith in Him. He then walked over to the coffin and commanded the young man to get up – and LIFE came back into his dead body! Jesus then delivered the boy back to his mother, as if to say, "Here is the answer to your prayers."

Jesus could have simply walked over to the casket and touch the coffin and stated "Get up!" But he had no Faith there that He could work with. The dead boy was "dead" - so his Faith was "dead" also. It wasn't going to help talking with the dead body... He needed the woman's Faith in order to do the miracle.

In your own life, if the Lord informs you to "do something" that appears so unimportant in your eyes - simply DO IT! Because when you follow Him in the little things, it allows Him to deal with the Faith which you simply demonstrated (just because He said to "do it') - and miracles will be the result!

Here in our study of the blind man sitting outside the gate, Jesus requires Faith to work with. Blind Bartimaeus had Faith enough to cry out to Jesus despite everyone around him telling him to be quite!

He received his healing because of his demonstration of his Faith. But this blind man had not demonstrated anything that would indicate he had put a demand on his Faith.

If you will check out the scriptures where people came to Jesus to be healed, often Jesus would ask them *"Do you have faith that I can do this?"* They would answer, *"Yes Lord!"*

And He would then state *"Let it be it done to you 'according to' your faith."*

In Luke chapter 17 verse 12 we see an example of Jesus healing the ten lepers. Much like with this blind guy, Jesus needed to tell them to go do something in conjunction with getting their healing; with the leprous men he stated *"Go and show yourself to the priest."* As they went, they were "walking by faith" and they were healed!

To this blind man, who had not shown any faith, Jesus stated *"Go wash in the pool of Siloam."*

He directed the blind guy to go all the way across town to dip in the pool of Siloam. When this man understood it was Jesus, he still didn't know what had been placed on his eyes. When Jesus said, *"go wash"* he obeyed. He probably thought it was some kind of eye salve or something. The point is – he did not know – but he went because Jesus told him to. Not understanding and still doing what you are commanded - is Faith!

When I was in the military, sometimes I would issue orders that I needed to be carried out immediately. I did not have time to explain "why" to those I had issued the orders to. I had "faith" my orders would be carried out and the men under me had "faith" that I would not issue an order unless it was important to be accomplished –

NOW! To my men – they demonstrated faith in me by following my orders without understanding the why. Once the situation was under control, I would always go back and explain the "why" to them. This cemented their "faith" in me, so next time they would have even "greater faith" in my orders.

This is why Jesus needed the blind man to "do what Jesus had told him to do," because it would produce Faith. The blind man did not know what was on his eyes or why he needed to go all the way across town to wash in that particular pool. But he believed Jesus would not have told him to do it if it was not important. So off he went!

Something else I want to point out. This blind man had never been able to clean himself enough to be allowed into the Temple area. When Jesus told him "go to the pool Siloam and wash," in the blind guy's mind, he seen himself as FINALLY being clean enough to go into the Temple location and offer sacrifices for his sins to God - something he had never been able to do in the past.

Considering that blind people were not allowed in the Temple area – but because Jesus had told him to *"go to the pool Siloam and wash"* - it all culminated in the mind of the blind guy that he was going to be healed and he was going to be cleansed and able to go inside the Temple area for the first time in his life! That built up the excitement in his spirit as he continued on his journey!

SELAH: There is (most of the time) a delay between the "AMEN" and "THERE IT IS!" It is during this time frame when you need to keep focused on the Word and promises that you have been given concerning whatever it is you are believing God for. Do not ever give up. There is no "formula" you can use to calculate the exact moment an answer to your prayer will materialize. I have had some prayers answered immediately while others took days, weeks, months and in some cases years (and some I am still standing in faith for – but I "know that I know" what the Lord has shown me – and I refuse to give up until I see the breakthrough)!

I heard Jerry Savelle teach on "having done all to stand, stand therefore..." He said someone once asked him, "Brother Jerry, how long do I have to stand there for?" His answer, "Until the answer comes!" When you are prepared to "stand forever" (if need be) – your answer will usually come pretty quickly – because the devil knows he just lost that battle. Amen!

So, whatever answer to prayer you are standing in Faith and believing God for – STAND until the victory comes!

Robert Thibodeau

CHAPTER FIVE

In the days of Jesus, the people that had physical deformities were seen as sinful or unclean (remember the concern the disciples asked Jesus, *"who sinned? This man or his parents that caused him to be born blind?"*) It was believed their deformity countered the purity of God and their presence in the Temple would defile the Temple. This is taught in Leviticus chapter 21 verses 17 to 21.

These scripture actually refers to limiting people that had any physical deformity from serving as priest. Through the centuries, however, the Jews took it to the extreme point where even physically healthy individuals were required to be washed clean prior to entering the Temple area even to worship! Not simply the priests - as outlined in the bible - but everybody! This ceremonial washing was done either at the pool of Siloam or at Solomon's Pool.

A blind man was not permitted to enter the Temple area until he was whole (healed). Blind people, cripples, etc. would send close friends or family members to the Temple in their place to make offerings for them. This was really dismaying for these people. They were told they were "not worthy" to go inside the Temple area. That is why individuals who were healed by Jesus were happy and so cheerful! They understood they were, once again, "righteous" in God's eyes (for healings were considered to be only attributable to God)!

So, when Jesus instructed the blind man to go and wash in the ritualistic pool at the entryway to the Temple - he understood what was about to take place! So every step he took across town - still blind - was increasing his faith in what Jesus had actually told him. He "saw" himself healed! Amen!

The Lord did not say for him to "go wash your eyes in some water" or to just simply "sprinkle some water on your face." That would not have worked because the custom of washing in the pool of Siloam suggested complete immersion, much like baptism today.

As I previously stated, this pool was all the way across town. The best estimates position this pool between half a mile and three quarters of a mile from where the man had actually been sitting outside the gate to the city. As we have previously discussed, his family had probably dropped him off that morning, so walking across town was not going to be a simple feat for the blind man to do. He probably asked for help and finally enlisted someone to escort him across town. Since he did not really trust the person he enlisted to help him, he would probably walk a little way and then ask someone, "Excuse me, where is the pool of Siloam? Which way do I go?"

And as they would direct him a little further down the roadway, definitely some people would have asked, "Why are you going to the pool Siloam? They may have even said, "There is a bath house over here that you can wash in..." (Due to the fact that they knew he would never ever be permitted to get in into the Temple complex because he was blind).

Now, using his Faith (remember, he can "see" himself

"seeing") he would have responded by stating something to the effect of, "No... Jesus the healer informed me to go clean my eyes in the pool of Siloam and I would be healed. So that's where I am going!"

He was probably mocked for saying things like that. Many times, as you are speaking out what you "see by Faith" – you will be mocked also. Do not let these times get you down! You are one step closer to receiving the answer to your prayers every time you take a step without seeing results... You are charging the atmosphere with Faith every time you speak Words that line up with what you are believing for but have not yet received.

As he continued walking, he would go a little further and the entire procedure would repeat itself, all the way across town. As he continued on his journey to the pool of Siloam and inform people why he was going there, he would repeat over and over exactly what Jesus had said to him. As he did that, he was also developing his Faith! It did not matter what other people believed or what they said. If they were laughing at him, it did not matter. He was bound and determined to go to the pool of Siloam! He was really "walking by faith!" Every halting step he took - he took by Faith. He had absolutely nothing but Faith in what Jesus said as he continued his walk across town, even with help.

But by FAITH, he finally arrived at the pool Siloam. I can just envision his enjoyment! As he was waiting in line, probably some of the people took a look at him and would have asked him, "You're blind! Why are you washing here? You don't belong here! Hey, what's that on your face?"

Their sarcasms did not bother him at all. He had made it to the pool of Siloam! He never wiped the clay off of his face. He never let anybody sidetrack him from completing his journey. He didn't care what they said or what they thought.

Some individuals there probably laughed at him. But, I am sure they were all watching carefully when, at last, it was his turn to get into the pool. He was still blind and probably needed to be led down the steps... And then he walked down into the pool and went under the water...

Just envision the thoughts he must have had as he sat there underwater. He was most likely enjoying the experience, since he had never had the ability to go there before! He was also most likely replaying over and over, as he was under the water holding his breath, what Jesus had said to him. 15 seconds pass... 20 seconds... possibly even 30 seconds go by as he is getting more excited about exactly what he is believing will take place!

The people standing around the pool were all leaning in and trying to get a better look. This fool of a blind man, coming to the pool of Siloam just because some insane rabbi informed him he might get his sight back by washing mud off of his face in the pool! Yet, even though they did not really believe it, they ALL wanted to see IF it would really happen!

The blind guy's whole life was soon to be changed - permanently! Then, as his ability to hold his breath was running out, he would have cleaned the clay off of his eyes - and stood up on his feet... I can just see him in my mind as he stands up - in the middle of the pool - with his face pointed up to heaven. I can see him as he cleans the water from his eyes. By Faith - and in obedience to the words of Jesus, he opens his eyes... and for the very first time - he sees that bright blue beautiful sky!

I can just imagine the joy he would have had! He would have let out a yell that was most likely heard half way across the city! He would have begun dancing and singing praises to God for the miracle that he just received! Oh, how he would have been carrying on!

He was probably making such a scene, with the people all praising and yelling and offering praises to God likewise, that the Temple Police would have responded to see what all of the turmoil was about. The Temple Police were responsible for keeping the peace so the Roman soldiers would not have to step in.

They would have shown up and asked, "What is going on here? Why are you making such a fuss? Settle down or you will have to leave!" He response would have been, "Why should I settle down? I am healed! Oh thank you God! I can see, I can see! I can see!"

He probably was making such a commotion (plus this occurred on the Sabbath day), the Temple Police hauled him off to the Temple Authorities telling him, "You can't act this way on the Sabbath Day! It's a violation of Temple Law!"

We can read in the John 9:8-12 that his neighbors (implying fellow Jews) knew about his lack of sight since birth. Without a doubt, some people there acknowledged him as "the blind guy who would sit outside pleading alms." Now, they see him walking around - and he sees them, too! Probably in astonishment, they were saying to one another as well as to the Temple Authorities, "Hey, isn't this the guy that was blind and sat by the roadside and asked alms of everyone?"

As he was brought in for questioning by the Temple Authorities, they would have seen his eyes looking normal and he would be looking at different things (bear in mind, this is the very first time he has actually seen the Temple itself)! The Temple Authorities knew that blind people have deformed or tarnished eyes. This guy's eyes were normal and everyone was giving testimony that he had "been born blind." They were now totally confused!

Some said, "This was the man!" Others were not so sure. The man who used to sit and beg for his entire life spoke out and emphatically proclaimed, "It's me! It's me!" Then everyone started to ask him the obvious question, "How did you receive your sight?"

And he replied, "A man named Jesus anointed my eyes with clay and told me to wash in the pool Siloam. So, I came - and I washed - and now I can see!"

It's appropriate to note this truth in the man's account. He did not discuss Jesus making the clay by spitting on the ground and putting that on his eyes. You might ask, "Why is that brother Bob?" The reason appears pretty clear to me... the blind guy had not seen what Jesus did. He just knew that Jesus had placed cold wet clay on his eyes. He didn't see that Jesus had actually spit on the ground and made the clay (he could not see what Jesus did). But this seemingly minor detail reveals the accuracy of God's word. Later, he does add this bit of information. More than likely, the person who escorted him across town had told him what had happened.

Those present now asked the man: "Where is Jesus, now?" They now understood Jesus was the one who had actually healed this guy - and had done so on the Sabbath day (which was an infraction of the Law). So now they wanted to arrest Jesus!

Apparently, Jesus had not followed the man to the pool. As far as Jesus was concerned, whether or not the man followed His orders and went all the way to the pool of Siloam and washed was completely on him. It was on his Faith alone... the Faith he had in doing exactly what Jesus instructed him to do, that the miracle would depend. Jesus wasn't going to lead him there - he had to go by Faith.

In response to the questioning of "Where is Jesus?" He

honestly did not know where Jesus was. **In John chapter 9 and verses 13 and 15, we read,**

"They brought to the Pharisees, him that before time was blind." **(John 9:13)**

Since it had been the Sabbath day when Jesus made the clay and opened his eyes, the Pharisees became involved. They were the "ultimate Temple Authorities." What the Pharisees said was, basically, The Law.

The Pharisees were required to investigate any claim of a miracle and the circumstances surrounding the miracle. Once the Pharisees understood this miracle involved Jesus (and that Jesus had done this act on The Sabbath Day), they wanted to arrest and question Jesus.

Once more, the Pharisees asked the once blind man how he received his sight. The man replied, *"He put clay on my eyes and I washed. Now I see."* **(John 9:15)**

SELAH: When you receive your "miracle," what are you going to do? Are you going to rejoice and let everybody know? Are you going to testify about the Power of God that gave you the breakthrough you have been waiting for? Or are you going to drift, quietly, back into the shadows and hope nobody notices?

When Jesus gives you the "petitions you have asked of Him" **(1 John 5:14-15)** – your job at that point is THREE FOLD:

1. Rejoice and give thanks!
2. Testify to others about what Jesus has done for you!
3. Lead others into a relationship with Jesus as well.

That way, THEY can have a miracle, too!

Chapter Six

John chapter 9:16, *"Therefore said some of the Pharisees, this man is not of God because he is not keeping the Sabbath day. And others said how can a man who is a sinner do such miracles? And there was a division among them."*

The miracle could not be denied. This guy, born blind, had actually received his sight when he complied with what Jesus told him to do. Some people present blatantly rejected him while others, being more sincere, concluded that a sinner could not do such miracles. As discussions continued, there was an obvious division between everyone that was there.

Throughout history, when Jesus is preached or taught, there will always be a division amongst those who hear about Him. You will certainly have those that believe as well as those that reject Him. Even in our politically correct Western society today, simply mentioning the

Name of Jesus brings a sharp division and reaction. Jesus was not politically correct when He was on earth and He has not been politically correct even to our day. He is in direct opposition to the atheistic society that is pervasive in America and in the western culture today. Today's cultural environment denies Godly moral principles while promoting every sin and upholding every perversion of man. Our government and our leaders in society are, in our day, rejecting Jesus in much the same way He was rejected when He was walking the earth.

His message is the same today. *"I tell you the Truth, but unless you repent you shall all likewise perish."*(**Luke 13:5)** Sinful people do not want to be rebuked of their sin and warned of the eventuality of their end in hell. For some reason, they get upset when informed they are going to hell unless they repent and change their wicked ways! You have to understand what Matthew records as Jesus' guidelines to His disciples, when He sent them forth to preach the kingdom, in **Matthew chapter 10 verses 33 through 35** (also, you can look at **Luke 12:8-9)**:

"Whosoever shall deny me before men, him will I also deny before my father which is in heaven. Don't think I have come to earth to send peace on earth, I did not come to send peace, but a sword. For I come to set a man at variance against his father and a daughter against her mother and a daughter-in-law against her mother-in-law."

Contrast that with what Jesus told the disciples about the coming of the comforter, the Holy Spirit, when He said,

"Peace I leave with you, my peace I give to you: not as the world gives, give I unto you. Let not your heart be troubled, neither let it be afraid " (**John 14:27**)**.**

The various responses to Jesus right here, in the text as well as here on the earth today, is that some believe in Him as the Holy Spirit brings conviction to their hearts, and some do not believe. Some people try so hard to shut their minds and hearts to the truth because it stands in the way of what they perceive as "their enjoyment" or "their right to do as they desire" - and they reject the Lord. They do not permit the truth to stand in the way of their unbelief!

It's interesting to keep in mind that those who reject Him almost always are greatly offended outwardly and respond with attacks meant to discredit Him, His teachings and His Word. Even today, their response shows that deep down, they do know the truth and they just refuse to confess or believe it honestly. Hence, they quench the convicting power of the Holy Spirit in a foolish attempt to validate themselves and their lifestyles.

You can see this in **John chapter 9:17** When the Pharisees speak to the blind man again,

"What do you say about him who has opened your eyes?" And he responded, *'He is a prophet."*

However the Jews did not believe (concerning him that had been blind and had actually received his sight)... until they called his parents to the Temple to question them as well. Again, they were attempting to discover some way to disprove what they understood to be true. They continued their interrogation of the man who had actually been blind (but could now see), by asking him again and again and again, exactly what Jesus had done to him. The formerly blind man responded, that in his opinion, Jesus was a prophet.

In Israel's history, it was only the prophets of God that used to talk with the people and do wonders or signs as proof they were sent by God. The clear ramification was that he, the formerly blind man who had been healed, believed Jesus was a prophet sent from God.

SELAH: When confronted with persecution for your faith, how do you respond? Are you prepared to give your testimony even when you know it will not be received? Are you prepared to face "whatever comes" rather than deny Jesus? The answer to those questions will determine the miracles you will see in your life.

Chapter Seven

John 9:19-23 - *"Is this your son who you say was born blind, how then does he now see? We know this is our son, we know he was born blind. How or by what means he now sees, we don't know. Or who has opened his eyes, we don't know. He is of age - ask him. He can speak for himself, And these words his parents spoke, because they feared the Jews: for the Jews had already agreed that if any man confesses that Jesus was the Christ he should be put out of the synagogue. Therefore his parents said, Ask him, he's of age."*

Still seeking to disprove the miracle, the Pharisees refused to believe that this man had been born blind. So they called his parents to continue the interrogation and asked them, "If he was born blind, how did he receive his sight?"

They tactfully replied that the man was their son and had been born blind. Whether they knew the details yet of how their boy had actually received his sight or not, they didn't say. In their defense, it was possible they did not know any more than their son had informed them of.

John records that the parents would not respond in more detail because the Jewish leaders had actually publicized they would cast any individual out of the synagogue if they confessed that Jesus was the Messiah. It could be that his parents, realizing the excellent miracle of their boy receiving his sight, also believed that Jesus was the Messiah. But they were not willing to publicly commit themselves to being believers, so they waffled in their support of their son.

John does not identify those the parents feared as being the Jewish rulers, but simply calls them "the Jews." This passage supplies strong proof of the technical use of the term, "the Jews." Doubtless the parents were Israelites, however they were not "Jews" in the sense of belonging to the ruling class. The title "the Jews" in this context was recognizing the hierarchical, ecclesiastical, political and ruling authorities and not the populous or basic general population of Israel.

Incorrect churches and Christian cults have always practiced excommunication as a method to regulate their members and keep their authority - even today. Our salvation is between an individual and God in the sacrifice of Jesus; and it is God who imparts redemption to each of us individually - through Jesus. It is everlasting and cannot be taken away by men if this redemption is truly received. God gives it to us in honor of the sacrifice Jesus made for us. If God were to favor the decisions of man – our eternal salvation would then be in the hands of man and not in the hands of Jesus.

Even God does not practice excommunication! Nor has God given any church leader or church, which biblically is just an assembly of believers, the authority to take away anybody's salvation. Ever!

"Now brother Bob, I thought excommunication was in the Bible. That we should be practicing this as a form of church discipline?"

It is true that churches can and need to practice church discipline, which if you study exactly what we're talking about here, implies breaking fellowship with members who are living in open sin and who refuse to repent. Church members who openly practice sin bring dishonor to the name of Christ and to the congregation. In order to return them to fellowship with the Lord and to not excuse their sin, the local church is instructed to dis-fellowship or break fellowship with them. This is plainly described in 1 Corinthians chapter 5, specifically the part of breaking fellowship in verses 9-13.

"I wrote unto you in an epistle not to keep company with fornicators: Yet not altogether with the fornicators of this world, or with the covetous, or extortioners, or with idolaters; for then must ye needs go out of the world. But now I have written unto you not to keep company, if any man that is called a brother be a fornicator, or covetous, or an idolater, or a railer, or a drunkard, or an extortioner; with such a one no not to eat. For what have I to do to judge them also that are without? Do not ye judge them that are within? But them that are without God judgeth. Therefore put away from among yourselves that wicked person."

However Paul then reaffirms his teachings on

excommunication and emphasizes that if the person repents of their wicked deeds and changes his ways, he can (and should) be accepted back into the fellowship (2 Corinthians 2:1-11).

"But I determined this with myself, that I would not come again to you in heaviness. For if I make you sorry, who is he then that maketh me glad, but the same which is made sorry by me? And I wrote this same unto you, lest, when I came, I should have sorrow from them of whom I ought to rejoice; having confidence in you all, that my joy is the joy of you all. For out of much affliction and anguish of heart I wrote unto you with many tears; not that ye should be grieved, but that ye might know the love which I have more abundantly unto you. But if any have caused grief, he hath not grieved me, but in part: that I may not overcharge you all. Sufficient to such a man is this punishment, which was inflicted of many. So that contrariwise ye ought rather to forgive him, and comfort him, lest perhaps such a one should be swallowed up with overmuch sorrow. Wherefore I beseech you that ye would confirm your love toward him. For to this end also did I write, that I might know

the proof of you, whether ye be obedient in all things. To whom ye forgive any thing, I forgive also: for if I forgave any thing, to whom I forgave it, for your sakes forgave I it in the person of Christ; Lest Satan should get an advantage of us: for we are not ignorant of his devices."

SELAH: Have you ever "judged" someone else based upon your interpretation of the Bible? Have you ever decided someone was so far gone into sin that you just "wrote him or her off" as destined to an eternal hell?

God does not tell us to become judges of who should and who should not go to Heaven or hell. He clearly instructs through the teachings of Jesus that our ONE AND ONLY JOB is to *"Go into all the world and preach the Gospel to every creature."* **(Mark 16:15).**

We should "plant the seed of the Gospel" into the hearts of men. By focusing on this one aspect of what our mission is – we can allow the Holy Spirit the free reign to develop that seed so it can become "fruit" for the Kingdom of God.

Chapter Eight

John 9:24-26, *"Then again, they called the man that was blind and said, "Give God the praise, we know this man is a sinner." And he answered and said, "Whether he's a sinner or not, I don't know. One thing I do know, before I was blind, now I see." They said again, "What did he do to you? How did he open your eyes?"*

Four times the Jewish rulers asked the man who was healed to discredit Jesus. What a paradox that they would advise the man to *"offer God the Praise"* for his healing ... but to brand Jesus (who was the means of the healing) as a sinner!

They could not reject the miracle that had happened. However, being blinded by their pride and self-righteous conceit, they refused to accept that it was Jesus who had actually healed him! To do so meant they would need to confess that Jesus' was the Messiah, the Son of God. Or at a minimum, to acknowledge He was a prophet sent by God... and then the people would question "why don't you listen to him then?"

Trying to label Jesus as being a sinner was meant to suggest Jesus truly had nothing to do with the healing. They based their whole condemnation of Jesus on the one point that He healed this guy on the Sabbath day. This man who was blind, but was now healed, had merely responded to what Jesus told him to do. He did not know whether Jesus was a sinner or not. But he absolutely knew he could now see! He had heard that anybody who came to Jesus that needed healing left healed! He had found the opportunity to be touched by Jesus; he believed what Jesus told him; and he had received his healing. In his mind, that was good enough to at least say, *"Jesus is a prophet!"*

Still seeking some type of justification for their attempts to discredit Jesus' character, they asked the man again, *"What did Jesus do? How did he open your eyes?"* **(John 9:26).**

It seems like they are attempting, frantically, to get the

man to state Jesus was the Messiah so they could kick him out of the synagogue. If they determined he was a heretic and worthy of being excommunicated, they could then discredit everything the man had said.

Most believers have the very same response to receiving redemption as the blind man did. Whereas the sinner is blind to God's Truth and salvation but then, through the miracle of redemption, their eyes are opened and they can see the facts as they are (they are sinners and headed to hell) and they ask Jesus to save them.

We cannot go through all the biblical realities to develop how God saves a sinner, (but we can say it is through Christ alone), but we can likewise not comprehend God's acts beyond what we do know.

Romans 5:8 states, *"but my God commends his love towards us, in that while we were yet sinners, Christ died for us."*

Can we truly fathom the love of God towards us? That He would send His only begotten Son from Heaven to this earth; to suffer, die and pay for the sins of the ones who sin against Him? The concern is rhetorical of course - and the answer is NO, we cannot genuinely comprehend the unlimited love of God that saves the sinner. We can be grateful and commend God for His mercy and His grace provided to us - through Christ Jesus our Lord!

It is challenging for a sinner to understand this while holding onto the sin. But when our eyes are open to the Truth and we believe we have received forgiveness, suddenly - we "can see." When we are truly born again and can look back at our "old life," only then are we able to stand in awe of God that, *"while we were yet sinners, Christ died for us!"* **(Romans 5:8)**

SELAH: Think. Think back to the "worst thing you have ever done." (Hint: Don't talk about it with anyone! Don't talk about it out loud and give the devil ammunition to use! Just think back to what this one thing was…). Then, think about the great LOVE God had for you – even when you did "that thing."

It does not matter what "it" was! Because if that "one

thing" would have been enough to keep the Blood of Christ from washing you so clean that the Father could forgive you – then the Blood of Christ was of no effect…it "wasn't good enough!"

But – Praise God! The Blood of Christ was not only "good enough" – it PERFECTLY paid the price for "that thing" you did that was so terrible in your mind.

For our promise is:

"Who his own self bare our sins in his own body on the tree, that we, being dead to sins, should live unto righteousness: by whose stripes ye were healed." **(1 Peter 2:24).**

Robert Thibodeau

Chapter Nine

John 9:27, *"He answered them and said, "I have told you already and you did not hear."*

Here, the former blind man (now healed) is answering their questions – again – that the Pharisees have continued to ask: *"How did he heal you?"* You can sense the frustration this man was experiencing. His responses to their continued interrogation of him are getting shorter and bolder. In John 9:27, he responds, *"I have told you already and you did not want to hear!"*

Or in other words *"You did not want to listen. Do you want me to say it all over again? Why do you want to hear it again? Will you also be his disciples?"*

And it's implied, *"If I do this again -* **will you become his disciples?"**

With this statement the Pharisees began to revile him and said, *"You might be his disciple, we're Moses' disciples, we know God spoke to Moses! As for this fellow, we don't know where he came from."* **(verses 28-29).**

I want you to notice something... each time this guy is questioned, his responses got better and better! That's the Holy Spirit bringing a Spirit of Boldness on him! This same blind man, who sat begging by the roadside, now is asking the elite religious scholars of Israel, "Why do you want to hear my testimony again?" And then added, *"Is it because you want to be his disciples?"*

There can be no question that this guy was rebuking them for their abstinence. His rebuke brought a swift response from his questioners as they began to *"revile him."* Which simply means that the tone of their questioning changed to being abusive and contemptuous as they implicated him of being Christ's disciple.

They responded they were Moses' disciples. They knew God had actually talked to Moses and gave to him The Law (The Ten Commandments). Then they stated that Jesus had actually just broken the Law by healing somebody on the Sabbath Day! Since Jesus had broken the Law, in their blinded eyes, He could not be from God. We can see the deceptiveness and bias in their statements.

Nicodemus saw Jesus' miraculous wonders and he said in John 3:2, *"We know you have come from God because no person could do these miracles unless God was with him."* Notice Nicodemus stated, *"We know..."* This suggests there has been some conversation going on in the Council and they have identified that Jesus is, undoubtedly, sent by God - otherwise He could not be doing these miracles.

If they were to publically confess this, it would cause a stir among the people and, more than likely, the Roman authorities would take some type of action against them. They could lose their influence over the people and a lot of their "extra income."

By "extra income" I am referring to a common accusation that some of the members of the Pharisees were operating a type of "black market," utilizing tactics much like the Mafia and other criminal elements do today. We can see an example of how this angered Jesus when He ran all the merchants out of the Temple complex and overturned the tables of the money changers **(Matthew 21:12).**

In my research, I have found some references that this incident is where they "decided Jesus had to die." To tie this to my reference of the Mafia operations of today, someone who causes them to lose money "must pay."

The sacrifices for the people had to be offered at the Temple. The Bible is very explicit in what animals were to be sacrificed and when. In order for one of these animals to be offered for the sins of the person or household, it first had to be inspected by the priests.

A family would have raised (for example) a lamb from birth, typically caring for it like we would a dog or cat today. It would have lived with the family, usually inside of the residence (to protect it from being marred in any way).

It was likewise a symbol of sacrifice due to the fact that it had come to be a "part of the family" during the year. Specifically in the eyes of youngsters, it would have become the "household pet." So when it came time to be offered for the sins of the household - the children actually had a great object lesson on what "sacrificial love" really implied. (Imagine if you had to offer "Fido" or "Fluffy" after getting them at about eight weeks of age and raising them in your house).

The kids would have loved their little pet…and now it is time to "offer it" as a sacrifice. For the youngsters, it would be hard. The older children would have come to accept it because they had experienced it repeatedly. But for the younger children, it would have been extremely hard. Then, to add to that stress, explaining to the youngsters that it was because they had been "bad" that "Fluffy" had to die! Now it became almost cruel! But, that is what life was like in ancient Israel.

When it came time for the Day of Atonement, the family would take a trip, commonly lasting several days (on hot, dusty roadways) before finally making it to Jerusalem and the Temple. As the father would take the animal to get inspected, a priest would almost always "find something" wrong with the animal.

At this point, the family had a choice to make. They might go all the way back home and try to raise another animal "without imperfection" and come back next year (and not have their sins forgiven for another year - which meant if any of them passed away, they would not have the guarantee of forgiveness and mercy of God and would be destined to an eternal hell); or they could go to the merchants and buy a "pre-approved" animal and offer that as the sacrifice. The merchant would offer to take the existing animal off their hands and would give them "trade in value" towards their purchase of another animal.

Once the family had actually purchased their pre-approved animal for sacrifice, they would go into the Temple location to await their turn for providing the sacrifice with the priests. Their initial animal would then be taken around back, washed up and put into the pen with other "pre-approved" animals to await the arrival of the next family.

It is rumored that the merchants and the priests were in cahoots together…and that the priests would get a "cut" of the profits from the deal…

Naturally, this was all "under the table" because if it became common knowledge, the people would rebel (or at least be complaining). If that happened and the Romans would find out, they would demand "their cut" or else they would arrest the offenders!

So, recognizing and declaring Jesus as being sent from God, was something the religious leaders just could not publicly accept. The cost was "too great" for them to make! We see the same understanding here and among the people in Luke 7 verse 16, when Jesus raised the son of the widow that we discussed previously. The scripture says a great fear came upon all of them, and they glorified God saying, *"A great prophet has risen up among us and God has visited his people."*

So there was absolutely no way the leadership of the Jews, and the Pharisees in particular, were ever going to publically agree with the once blind man that Jesus was a prophet sent from God. No way! Ever!

That left them with their only other option – discredit the healed man and, in effect, discredit Jesus in the eyes of the people.

SELAH: Religious tradition! How powerful those two words are. Religious tradition will STOP the Blessing from working in your life! Just because you attend a church that does not "believe in healing" does not mean God does not heal. I can guarantee you, if you needed healing (from cancer or some other life threatening illness, for you or your child or other loved one) – and you went to your pastor for prayer and was told, "Sorry, we don't believe healing is for today..." – I GUARANTEE YOU – you would be looking for another church - QUICK!

That is how Christian missionaries are making an impact in Muslim countries. If they go in and hold a "revival" meeting – they could be arrested (or worse). But, if they go in to hold a "conference" with other Christian pastors – and "word gets out" that they will be praying for the sick at this conference – it is packed out!, Usually it is with Muslim women bringing their children to be prayed for. I have a very good friend who has a mighty ministry in Muslim and Hindu areas. He preaches THE WORD at these conferences – then prays for the sick and *"the Lord working with (the Word that was preached) and confirming the Word with signs following!"* (Mark 16:21). He has told me that a Muslim woman who receives her child back from almost certain death is now also open to receive the Lord as her Savior... and another seed is planted into that dark kingdom of Islam.

Don't let your own religious traditions or unfounded beliefs get in the way of your miracle! Especially do not let your traditions get in the way of someone else receiving Jesus as their Savior. If you are satisfied with attending a non-believing church – go ahead. But do not "look down" on someone who wants to take his or her faith to the next level!

Chapter Ten

John chapter 9:30-33 – *"The man answered and said unto them, Why herein is a marvelous thing, that ye know not from whence he is, and yet he hath opened mine eyes. Now we know that God heareth not sinners: but if any man be a worshipper of God, and doeth his will, him he heareth. Since the world began was it not heard that any man opened the eyes of one that was born blind. If this man were not of God, he could do nothing."*

This man is plainly being led by the Holy Spirit and begins to boldly preach to the self-righteous Jewish leaders. He points out the clear absurdity of their denying that Jesus was from God. These were not just oblivious commoners, but the elite of Israel! These were the folks who were the most superior in knowledge and position in Israel. Yet this beggar (without any official training) reveals their conceit and exposes their unwarranted prejudice against Jesus.

The man brilliantly presents a vital principle of biblical analysis. Any conclusion as to the definition of a biblical event or statement must be analyzed in the analogy of the Faith. He did this by mentioning the irrefutable reality that God does not listen to sinners and suggests God cannot bless, hear or be a party to, the works of a man unless the work is in line with God's concepts. And this man reminds them that Isaiah prophetically stated, speaking of the latter days, in *Isaiah 35: 5-6*:

"Then the eyes of the blind shall be opened, the ears of the deaf shall be unstopped. Then shall the lame man leap as a Hart, and the tongue of the dumb sing: for in the wilderness shall waters break out, and streams in the deserts."

Many times Isaiah refers to the spiritually blind and deaf as having their ears opened to God's truth, as we can see in **Isaiah 29:18***:*

"And in that day shall the deaf hear the words of the book, and the eyes of the blind shall see..."

But in chapter 35, the context is plainly addressing the physical blessings that God would give Israel and the promised kingdom, the millennium. The context for chapters 32 to 36 is explained in Isaiah 31 (which we will not go into here for the sake of time and space but is worth your time to read in your own Bible study time). *Chapters 32 to 36* begins the discourse of messianic prophecy, with this statement:

"Behold a King shall reign in righteousness and a Prince shall rule in judgment." **(Isaiah 32:1).**

The King is the guaranteed coming Messiah. Isaiah prophesied of the terrific miracles and prosperity that would go along with the coming Messiah. The Pharisees were aware of this prophecy. They just refused to believe it was Jesus!

But to me, the wonder of the once blind man's statement is that he was apparently knowledgeable about God's promises and the scriptural historians of Israel were not! One thing he reminded the Rabbi's of was that never in history had a guy who had actually been born blind received his sight. Only God could bring that kind of healing to a blind man's eyesight. Thus, there were no premises for their statements that Jesus was a sinner and that God was not with him.

AND THEY GOT MAD! Right there, this ignorant beggar rebuked them – PUBLICALLY! And it went straight to their hearts! They were not going to sit there and allow an uneducated beggar talk to them like that! They addressed him in verse 34,

"You were altogether born in sin and now you're trying to teach us!"

And they cast him out...

As I mentioned previously, the response of the carnal heart when exposed for what it truly is, is to personally assault the one who reveals the mistake. It is obvious the rulers did not listen to the man's statements, but evaluated the man according to their traditions as one who was born in sin. In their viewpoint, he did not deserve to even stand in front of them... and definitely was not deserving to advise them of what the scriptures said or meant! They presented themselves as the spiritual leaders of Israel. That expression "born in sin" was condemning and refers back to John 9:2, which was the initial concern that the disciples had asked Jesus about.

They implied that this man was a vile sinner who had sinned in some preexistent life or whose parents had sinned in some way - thus disqualifying him from having any spiritual insight to address them who were the "religious leaders" of Israel. So their response was to immediately excommunicate him from the Synagogue. This meant that he was now ostracized from Jewish society as well. He was, in effect, an outcast.

They effectively branded the man as the worst of the worst sinners and unfit to be among the rest of the Jews. In verses 35 to 38, we see Jesus heard they had cast him out of the Synagogue and when he found him, Jesus said to him,

"Do you believe on the Son of God? And he answers and said, "Who is He, Lord, that I might believe on him?" And Jesus said to him, "You both seen Him and He it is that talks with you." And he said "Lord I believe!" And he worshiped Jesus."

SELAH: When you take a stand you know is right – and then receive persecution for it – will you back down? It might be an ethical decision you make at work and your boss threatens to fire you unless you "go along" with the situation. What are you going to do?

So many people today believe the lie "everybody is doing it – so it must be ok." Just because "everybody is doing it" does not make it "ok" in God's eyes. I seen something recently that read, "Just because the government says it is ok does not make it ok in God's eyes." You can just study Sodom and Gomorrah as examples. God does not "change His ways" just to satisfy the "whims of the people."

There are many things regarded as "normal" or "it's our right" in today's culture that are not accepted in God's Kingdom. As a member of the Body of Christ and as a member of the Family of God and part of the Kingdom of God on this earth…it should not be ok for you either.

Persecution will come when you take your stand as an Ambassador for Christ. When it does come, how will you react? Will you react like this man did? He refused to back down – and it cost him dearly in the natural.

But, when Jesus heard what had happened, He "sought him out" – and this man was one of the very few people on earth that Jesus personally ministered to and told him that he was The Christ – The Messiah!

If your Christian Faith costs you in the natural, remember what Jesus said in **Luke 18:29-30:**

"And he said unto them, Verily I say unto you, There is no man that hath left house, or parents, or brethren, or wife, or children, for the kingdom of God's sake, Who shall not receive manifold more in this present time, and in the world to come, life everlasting."

Robert Thibodeau

Chapter Eleven

John 9:35-38

"Jesus heard they cast him out and when he found him, he said to him, "Do you believe on the Son of God? And he answered and said who is He Lord, that I might believe on him?" And Jesus said to him, "You both seen him and he it is who talks with you." And he said, "Lord I believe!" And he worshiped him, (he worshiped Jesus)."

Excommunication was a major, serious matter in Israel. It was also done openly so as to be a warning to others. It could most likely be presumed that the man was somewhat distraught over what had actually happened (being excommunicated). Even understanding that he was right, he had no concept of what Jesus looked like or where he might find Him. Once again, we see this man putting himself into a position or location, where Jesus could discover him - again. And, once more, Jesus does just that - He finds somebody who is "looking for Him." Jesus verifies in this guy's eyes and in his mind (and permanently in his spirit) that Jesus is the Son of God, the long awaited Messiah.

Jesus heard exactly what had transpired and, in front of His disciples and others, Jesus publicly showed His compassion for the man and went to where the man was in order to minister to him. Jesus' concern for this man perfectly and absolutely represents God's plan of salvation. Jesus simply asked him a direct question,

"Do you believe on the Son of God?"

Jesus did not ask the man what religious works he has done or what he had accomplished in his life. He did not even ask about the man's character or about his past. Jesus just asked a question,

"Do you believe?"

It was baffling to the blind man that the Pharisees (after seeing and also verifying Jesus' miracles), would question whether Jesus was from God or not!

Numerous churches and spiritual leaders today also neglect the reality the Bible plainly teaches, that "redemption is by faith alone," apart and separate from works. Jesus went to this man to advise him on how he could be saved.

If salvation was of belief *plus* works (such as baptism, church membership, sacraments, or any other rights or religious acts), why didn't Jesus go and explain this to the man? The answer is simple: Redemption is by faith (and in faith alone), by believing in the Son of God, who offers believers redemption, forgiveness of sins and eternal life - as His totally free gift!

Ephesians 2 verses 8-9 says,

"For by grace you are saved through faith; and that not of yourselves: it is the gift of God: not of works, lest any man should boast."

Jesus Himself said to Nicodemus in **John 3,** when He instructed him on how to be born again,

(16) "For God so loved the world that He gave His only

Son that whosoever would believe in him should not perish but have everlasting life...(36) He that believes on the Son has everlasting life; and he that believes not the Son shall not see life; but the wrath of God abides on him."

The man asks Jesus *"Who is the Son of God so I can believe in him?"* There could be no question here that Jesus demonstrated his Deity to the man. Jesus said to the man that he was actually looking at the Son of God and that it was He who was speaking to him. The man now, both *spiritually and physically*, was seeing Jesus the Messiah! And he believed! Keep in mind the fact that this man had actually been born blind. He had been blind his whole life. As we already discussed, this guy's senses developed to the point that he was intensely aware of everything going on around him.

I believe this guy immediately recognized the voice of Jesus as the one who had healed him. So when Jesus started talking with him and informed him He was the Son of God, any Jewish boy worth his salt would recognize that person as the Messiah! It was the

Messiah who was talking to him! This guy's response was the best proof of true salvation (for him, for you, for me or for anyone), in that he immediately began to worship Jesus.

This guy, though not officially trained, was advised enough in the matters of God to understand that you are to praise only the One True God. Any man whose eyes are spiritually open to who Jesus is will certainly always bow before Him!

SELAH: Have you ever had one of those "AH-HA" moments? When you have been told something (perhaps over and over) and you just "don't get it?" Perhaps you know the basics and you can give mental assent to the precepts…but then, suddenly…you "get it!"

I know I have experienced some things like that. An example, for me is Algebra. I was never very good at it in high school. I continued to put off College Algebra until the very end when I "had to take it." But, after just a few days in class – I "got it!" I remember thinking to myself, "Why couldn't I understand this stuff years ago?"

Spiritually, you may have been brought up in the church your entire life (I know I was). But there comes a day, when you "get it." When suddenly, all the "lights turn on" and you understand who Jesus really is and what He has already done – FOR YOU. Not for some blind man over 2,000 years ago – but FOR YOU, today! When that happened – you experienced EXACTLY what this man experienced on that day he was "kicked out of Jewish society" for standing up for Jesus. He did not understand who Jesus really was – he just knew that the charges being made against Jesus did not make sense.

When Jesus found him later and revealed Himself to this man – he had one of those "AH-HA" moments! You experienced the same realization this man experienced on that day.

When you witness to someone and the "lights come on" for them – they experience the same "AH-HA" moment that you, this man and every other born again believer experiences when they realize "whom Jesus really is!"

Our job is to share Jesus with everyone until that "AH-HA" moment arrives for them!

Robert Thibodeau

Chapter Twelve

John 9:39-41 *"For judgment I came into this world, that they which see not might see; and that which see might be made blind. And some of the Pharisees, which were with him heard these words and said to him, "Are we blind also? Jesus said to them, 'If you were blind, you should have no sin: but now you say 'We see;' therefore, your sin remains.'"*

When Jesus ministers to the man who was blind (but was now healed), He did not do it in private (as verse 40 shows). The man was excommunicated publicly. Now, Jesus is going to justify him publicly. The Pharisees accused the man of being "outside the will of God" publicly. Now, Jesus was going to publicly expose the Pharisees as being outside of the will of God.

Listening on the sidelines (as He was ministering and speaking to the once blind man) were some of the

Pharisees. These Pharisees heard Jesus' words which He had spoken to the healed man.

I believe it was for the benefit of the Pharisees that Jesus mentioned that He had not come to bring judgment, but to open the eyes of the spiritually blind. It's fascinating to me that the spiritual leaders, who had railed on Jesus for days trying to belittle Him and embarrass Him, were about to be exposed for the Spiritual blindness they truly had in their hearts. However Jesus, in His mercy and His grace, reveals to these men that He, the Messiah, has not come to judge them and condemn them, but to reveal them the reality, the Truth and the fulfillment of the actual Scriptures they believed.

Once again, their response exposes their real spiritual condition, because with terrific self-righteousness and pride, they ask, *"Oh, are we all blind too?"*

You can often see this kind of blindness manifest in false spiritual leaders and cults today. When the Truth of the Word is presented, they become offended and begin to lash out at the one exposing their sinfulness.

In their pride, these Pharisees considered themselves to be far superior to other men. After all, they were the ones who were educated and were held up as the spiritual leaders of the Jews. Even in American and Western churches today, there are some who think their position (at least in their own minds) puts them far above any question or possibility of being in error. Often they will surround themselves with a staff that insulates their "leader" from the "common folk" and this just reinforces the deception. The illustration I once heard will fit perfectly here:

"It's commonly said that if a rock is tossed into a pack of dogs, the dog that is hit is the one who howls!" Amen!

That is what happens when you use the Word of God to bring correction to someone who's living a deceived life or lifestyle. They will "howl" because they have been hit with the "Rock" (Jesus)!

Jesus said to them, *'If you were blind you should not have sinned, but now you say 'we see,' therefore your sin remains."*

Ooh, this upset them! In other words, "They were mad!"

They believed they were above sin and Jesus' candid response to that question was, *"yes they were blind."* He explained that, due to the fact they denied they were sinners; they were guilty of their sin. This provides another vital part of how salvation is received. When an individual admits to being a sinner, only then will he see the need for forgiveness and the requirement for God's Grace and Mercy. The self-righteousness and the self-confident believe in their own worthiness of God's favor. Therefore, they see no need of God's Grace.

Jesus had actually just informed this man, who had been healed of blindness, that salvation was by Faith in Him, as the Son of God. The Pharisees rejected Jesus as the Messiah, the Son of God.

Friend, Jesus has currently done all the battling, delivering, healing and all the saving that He is going to do. He provides us, His church, His Body (the followers living on the earth at this time) the power to do exactly the very same things that He did while He was on this earth. In fact, Jesus stated we should be doing even greater works than that which He did. (John 14:12)

Can you imagine being able to do things even Jesus could not do? That would be quite an anointing to walk in! That's the specific kind of anointing that Jesus stated we must walk in while we remain on this earth! So the question is, are you walking in that kind anointing today? And if not, why not?

We need to have what I call *"Blind Faith"* (and hence, the title of this book). If you can trust Him to save you, then you can trust Him to heal you, too. If he can heal you – then it would fairly simple for him to provide for you financially as well. There is nothing that Jesus cannot do – if you have the Faith to believe it! Sometimes, we do not understand "how" He can do it…and it is at times like this that we need to have **"Blind Faith!"**

When you get to that point, and only then, will you be able to share the scriptures with someone else and have their total, concentrated and complete interest - because you have lived it.

It is not just something you "heard about." You actually "experienced" that kind of deliverance and that kind of provision. That kind of Salvation! You will be able to explain that you "experienced" being born again. This makes you well qualified to share that experience with others.

This is our only purpose and our only goal:

To share the Gospel of Salvation with as many people as possible!

SELAH: When you were born again, you probably were excited and wanted to share that information with those you love (and, if you were like I was, everyone else around you, too)! Has that "Holy Fire" began to cool off in your life? If so, you need to "stoke the Fire" to get it roaring HOT again!

How do you do that? By making a quality decision to spend additional time in the Word of God on a DAILY BASIS. I am not talking about "hours per day" (though IF you did that – I can guaranteed you – you WILL be Blessed for it). I am saying you need to begin "where you are at."

If you would simply get up 30 minutes earlier than you do now... put the coffee pot on, grab your Bible and read just ONE CHAPTER each day (while you are waiting for the coffee to finish brewing) – you will gain a deeper relationship with God than you could ever imagine. Why? <u>Because you are making the decision to spend time with Him</u>... it is your "alone time" with the Creator of the Universe! It is your "appointment" with Him! You are honoring God when you do that... and when you honor God – He returns the Favor!

Some people enjoy reading their Bible just before they go to bed. Which ever is right for you is for you and God to discuss. But you need to begin doing this on a DAILY basis. Start NOW – don't even wait (like most people) "until Monday" to begin to make a change. Make the commitment to God and to Jesus that you will begin NOW, today, to spend quality time with Him in His Word.

It is the best gift you can give yourself – to spend time with God!

Robert Thibodeau

Chapter Thirteen

Conclusion

As we go through our daily toils in this life, sometimes we are unaware of the needs of those around us. We get so caught up in the everyday issues of "our life" that we forget we have a mission and a purpose for being here. God has a need for each and every believer on planet earth – right now.

We may not always get it right. But if we are quick to repent of our sins and plead the Blood of Jesus over our sins – God the Father honors the Blood and looks at us as if we have never sinned. It does not matter what you have done – NOTHING can stop the Blood of Jesus from working in your life.

Throughout this book, I have included little areas at the end of each chapter to just spark your thoughts… the Biblical term is "Selah" which means, "to pause and to think about…"

If you would just "slow down" and "Selah" things in your

life as they pertain to God (or, in some cases, do not pertain to God – in which case you need to repent and make some necessary changes in those areas), things would go along so much better. Most of the time, mistakes <u>we make</u> along the way tend to destroy us. But if we truly repent of these sins, God is faithful and just to forgive us of our sins. He is more than able to make a way when there is no way!

I have personally met a man who was convicted of terrible crimes and sent to prison. While in prison, he murdered other inmates and was looking at spending the rest of his natural life in prison. His "nickname" in prison was "Mad Dog" (and it fit). But that was BEFORE he was saved!

But, he became born again and was turned onto God! His total attitude changed while he was still in prison. He did not "get out" and then find God…no – he found God while in the darkest, deepest, worst pit that a person can dwell in. But, even in that environment, he found Faith in God and received Jesus as His Savior.

That, in itself is a miracle worth repeating! Several years later, God provided Grace and Mercy for him and he was released from prison. In the natural, there was no reason for him to be released back into society.

But God...

As soon as he was released, he began to follow through on his commitment to God. He and his wife, entered the ministry. It was hard at first...he had lived most of his life in prison. He was "rough" around the edges (not to mention with other people)! He had a hard time "shaking" habits that had been drilled into him. Habits that had become his way of life. Habits he depended on in prison for survival.

But the Love of God had been shed abroad in his heart...and through the course of a couple of years both he and his wife seen, lived and observed God's supernatural provision as they served Him with all they had and with all of their being.

Then, almost out of nowhere, they found themselves, of all places - at Bible School! He had dedicated himself to the Lord in prison and God had arranged for him to get out. He was simply following through on his commitment to the Lord that he would go through every open door if it meant he could share the Gospel with those that needed to hear it.

You see - the person who committed all of those terrible crimes and spent years of his life in prison was not the same person anymore after he was born again. Second Corinthians 5:17 states, *"Therefore, if a man be in Christ, he is a NEW creature (a NEW creation); old things are passed away; behold, all things are become new."*

When Bear Morgan (the man I am talking about), became born again – the "old Mad Dog Morgan" died (spiritually). A "new man" was instantly born. A new man that loved God and all he wanted to do from that point on was to serve God with all he had.

By the way, his new nickname "Bear" was actually shortened from "Teddy Bear" (it seems "Teddy Bear" might not be a very good nickname while locked away in one of the worst of the worst prison systems)! So he dropped the "Teddy" part and shortened it to "Bear."

A few years after he was released from prison, he attended - and graduated - from Jerry Savelle's Bible School in Crowley, Texas (that is where I met him).

After graduation, he and his wife, Dove Morgan, continued their motorcycle and prison ministry and made significant impact in the prison world and biker world. They could go places most ministers could not go. They knew the "lingo" and they knew the environment. Their ministry and their testimony are still talked about today.

Although Bear has gone on now to be with the Lord, Dove continues to serve the Lord in the ministry she and Bear started, "Loving Hearts Ministry." She has since relocated from Texas to Oklahoma, but the ministry is still going strong! (For more information on Dove Morgan and her ministry, please visit her website at http://lovingheartsministry.org But, the point I am making is this:

When you receive Jesus as your Lord and Savior – ALL THINGS are possible! Matthew 19:26 reads, *"With men, this is impossible: but with God – ALL*

things are possible."

That does not mean there will never be any more problems in your life. The devil will see to it that when you start to *"walk by faith and not by sight,"* you will be tested. You will face things you never thought or imagined could happen. But, if you stand fast in your faith – you have the assurance that Jesus will see you through.

We studied about the man who was born blind. His entire life he heard that "he or his parents had committed some kind of sin and now he is paying the price for it." But when Jesus told those disciples that *"he had not sinned, nor had his parents"* (Jesus was not talking about "they have never sinned," i.e. *sinless* – the simple meaning here is there was no sin in his life which caused the blindness), this man's HOPE came alive.

"Could that be the case?" he was asking himself. "If that's the case, then God could still have a plan for my life." It was this type of Faith that Jesus was going to use to effect the healing. But, that healing came at a cost.

The man ended up being ridiculed and excommunicated from the Temple (which effectively ostracized him from Jewish society). He was now "worse off" (naturally speaking) than when he was blind! But, he refused to waiver in his support, his Faith and his belief in Jesus.

This caused Jesus to search him out, and to personally minister to him the plan of salvation. You do not read about very many people who Jesus revealed Himself to as the Son of God (i.e. Messiah) prior to the Cross and His Resurrection. There were only a handful of people who had that kind of intimate knowledge about Him. This man was one person who was in that select group.

Why would Jesus reveal Himself to this man in that manner? Because this man had "given up all" in his allegiance to Jesus. In Matthew 19:29, Jesus said, *"...every one that has forsaken houses, brethren, sisters, father, mother, wife, children or lands for my name's sake, SHALL RECEIVE an hundredfold and shall inherit everlasting life!"*

This man, blind since birth, had heard about the healing anointing on a man called Jesus. He wanted to meet him so badly. He had heard about other blind people who had come to Jesus and they ALL were healed. But, whoever this man had escorting him to the city gate each day (so he could beg for alms), obviously refused to take him to Jesus.

But, one day, Jesus came to him. His life changed forever on that day. On the surface, it looked like it had turned for the worse. Despite the initial victory in gaining his sight, he ended up being kicked out of the Temple and was considered an outcast from Jewish society. Even his parents refused to back him up.

"But Jesus..." - oh, how I love that phrase! Here was a man who refused to follow social norms and acceptance. He refused to go back on his claim that Jesus was an anointed man sent from God. He was given Holy Spirit inspired insight into the scriptures – and actually presented a compelling argument in behalf of Jesus before the religious leaders of that day! This is what caused him to be excommunicated. When Jesus heard what had happened to the man (and why), He could not let faith like that waiver...

When you decide to take a stand for Jesus – a "no matter what, I'm not backing down" type of stand – Jesus will also "come to where you are at" and minister to your needs as well. If you refuse to deny Him – He will never deny you.

My friend, if you have never received Jesus as your Lord and Savior – I urge you to do so today. Turn the page, read - and then PRAY – the short, simple prayer provided. Do just as the blind man did - simply believe!

Well, Brother Bob, how can I know that God will hear me? And if He hears me, how do I know that He will forgive me? You don't know what I've done in my life!"

That is correct…I do not know what you have done in your life. I don't need to know and neither does anyone else! Take that to God. Jesus, through His death on that cross, died for YOU! God accepted His sacrifice in your place! He honored Jesus by raising Him from the dead and He promised He would honor you if you would simply believe He honored Jesus by raising Him from the dead.

You can read that for yourself in Romans chapter 10

versus 9,10,13:

"...if you will confess with your mouth the Lord Jesus and shall believe in your heart that God has raised Him from the dead, you shall be saved. For with the heart man believes unto righteousness; and with the mouth confession is made unto salvation. For whosoever shall call upon the name of the Lord shall be saved!"

In First John chapter 5, versus 14-15, you have the assurance that God the Father will hear your prayer:

"And this is the confidence we have in Him, that, if we ask anything according to His will, He hears us: and if we know He hears us, whatsoever we ask, ***we know that we have the petitions that we desire of Him."***

There is only ONE THING separating you from Eternal Life with Jesus and God the Father...and that ONE THING – is <u>YOU</u>!

God has done all that He is going to do to provide you a way to receive the forgiveness of everything you have ever done wrong, thought wrong or lived wrong... He provided Jesus.

Jesus lived a perfect life in this earth and died in your place. So Jesus has also done all He is going to ever do to provide you a way to receive the forgiveness of everything you have ever done wrong, thought wrong or lived wrong…**He paid your debt to God.**

The only thing left for you to do is to *"confess with your mouth and believe with your heart"* that Jesus really did do that for YOU! And to believe that God the Father honored that sacrifice for YOU and raised Jesus from the dead.

When you come to the place where you can do that, you have entered into the Life of Faith!

After that first step (from death onto Eternal Life with God the Father and Jesus as your Lord and Savior) you are now ready to begin to live your life for Him. You are now ready to begin

"Walking by Faith

To Receive What You Cannot See!"

That is

"Blind Faith"

Be Blessed in ALL That You Do!

Robert Thibodeau

Freedom Through Faith Ministries

Baltimore, Maryland

April, 2015

A Sinners Prayer for Salvation

If you have never asked Jesus to forgive you of your sins; if you have never before acknowledged Him as the Son of God who was sent by God the Father into this earth to pay the price for the sinfulness of man; or - if you are a Christian but have left the Faith and walked in worldliness and now want to repent of that sinful past and return to a loving relationship with Jesus – pray this short prayer from your heart:

Jesus, I know I'm a sinner and I know I don't deserve heaven. I don't deserve God's love, but I believe your Word, that God loves me and gave you to die in my place; that you love me and gave yourself and your life for me... I believe that, Jesus. So, right now, I ask you - Jesus, to come into my heart and to become Lord over my life. Wash me clean of all my past sins. Thank you, Jesus for giving your life for me... now, Lord, I give to you, my life. Lord, make your abode in my heart. Jesus, I praise you for saving me. I declare before Heaven and Earth that you are my King and you are my Savior. From this point forward Jesus, I trust in you and you alone. Father God, Thank You for loving me that much. Jesus, thank you for giving to me your Righteousness in the eyes of the Father. Thank you for making me a "child of the Living God, heir of God and a joint heir with you!" (according to Romans 8:17).

I pray this prayer in Jesus Name – Amen!

Now, let me be the first to say, **"Welcome to the Family!"** Amen! You are NOW in the Family of God!

Do me a favor and drop me a line or email and let me know that you prayed that prayer. I want to rejoice with you, pray for you and, if you send me your contact and postal delivery information, I have some information I want to send out to you absolutely free of charge! This information will help you to take the "first steps" of your new - Eternal Life!

Pastor Bob

ABOUT THE AUTHOR

Pastor Robert Thibodeau (Pastor Bob) is the Founder and Director of **"Freedom Through Faith Ministries"** *(FTFM.org)* and is actively involved with our outreach ministry called **"Mission For America."**

Mission For America is a Spiritual Warfare Ministry. Pastor Bob holds public (usually outdoor) prayer meetings in specific geographic and spiritually symbolic locations around this nation. He then prays against and binds "demonic powers, wicked spirits in high places, rulers of the darkness of this world and against princes and principalities and powers in the air" (Ephesians 6:12) that are operating in the spiritual atmosphere of this nation and influencing leaders at all levels, both elected and appointed.

He then prays for the leaders of this land and prays for their salvation and leads the prayer of Second Chronicles 7:14. Pastor Bob then leads the public proclamation that "Jesus is Lord over the United States of America!" These meetings are video taped, edited and then placed on YouTube and also on the "Mission For America" website *(www.mission4america.com)*.

Pastor Bob is also the Founder / Director of the **"Freedom Through Faith Radio Network"** (www.FTFRadioNetwork.com). FTFRN has three radio stations currently playing 24 hours per day.

Freedom Through Faith Christian Radio (FTFCR) is currently rated in the TOP 4% of all online Christian Talk / Sermon radio stations in the world, with listeners in over 130 different countries. Through this online radio station, smaller ministries have an opportunity to minister the Word of God to the World on an offering basis (no set fees).

This allows us to *"Empower Others to Impact Their World with the Gospel of Jesus Christ."* Any ministry desiring to broadcast their recorded programs on FTFCR may set the offering price they value their own program at...even $1 per month! No other ministry offers this type of national and international exposure on an offering basis! For more information, please visit the station website at www.FTFChristianradio.com

The **"Praise and Worship Radio"** station plays a full spectrum of Christian music genre 24 hours per day. "Praise and Worship Radio" is rated in the Top 5% of all online Christian music stations in the world, with listeners in over 150 countries! We allow independent Christian artists and musicians the opportunity to play their music on our station for a one time offering of just $5. This allows their music to be heard world wide up to 4 times per day - everyday - with no additional offerings required. For more information, please visit our website at www.FTFRadioNetwork.com

"Evangelism Radio" is our latest online radio station. This station is designed to support *LIVE BROADCAST MINISTRY* - 24 hours per day! Almost one year in development and testing, Evangelism Radio allows those ministries desiring to enter *LIVE BROADCAST MINISTRY* to do so at very affordable rates. For just $10 per month, a ministry may broadcast LIVE one 30 minute broadcast each week; our most expensive plan allows a ministry to broadcast LIVE 60 minutes each day and every day - 7 days per week - for only $80 per month!

"Evangelism Radio" also has its own phone line support that allows a broadcaster, from anywhere in the nation, to have their listeners call in LIVE and interact with the broadcaster. This phone support is provided FREE to the broadcaster (though some listeners calling in may have to pay for long distance charges if they are not using VOIP technology - but there is NO CHARGE to the broadcaster).

After just one year of operations, **Evangelism Radio** is consistently ranked by ShoutCast.com in the Top 10 Sermon genre Internet radio stations in the world with over 6,000 listener hours each month!

In addition, beginning in January 2015, **Evangelism Radio** is now "simulcast" over **Freedom Through Faith Christian Radio** – 24 hours per day! This means our broadcasters are heard on two major Internet radio stations around the world – for no additional charges!

For more information, on becoming a broadcaster with our radio ministry, please visit our website at www.evangelismradio.com

More information on the **"Freedom Through Faith Radio Network,"** and detailed information on all three of our radio stations, please visit our website at www.FTFRadioNetwork.com.

Robert Thibodeau

Special Meetings

and

Invitations to Speak:

Pastor Bob's unique style of preaching includes lively, spiritual lessons, straight from the Word of God. He always includes a special prayer session for the sick and those needing healing or deliverance. In these prayer sessions, God confirms the Word just preached with signs and miracles.

These meetings are held on an offering basis for both large groups and small churches. Pastor Bob has preached in services with only 5 people and also in sessions involving 5,000 attendees. But he preaches with the same intensity and Love of God for both small and large.

There are no set fees for Pastor Bob to come and minister to your group, church or special meeting. All we ask for is the opportunity to accept a love offering for our ministry and the ability to sell books and CD's in the lobby or designated area before and after the service.

It is important to note that Pastor Bob receives NO salary or other compensation from this ministry. ALL offerings go directly to work in assisting Pastor Bob and this ministry in our Mission to "Get The Word Out!"

To schedule Pastor Bob, or to receive more information on his ministry, please visit our main website at www.FTFM.org

BE BLESSED IN ALL YOU DO!

Freedom Through Faith Ministries

PO Box 4936

Baltimore, MD 21220

www.FTFM.org

Other books by Pastor Robert Thibodeau

(All books are available through Amazon, Barnes & Noble, Kindle and from the ministry website)

"7 Keys to Answered Prayer"

"The Six Trials of Jesus"

"The Marriage Ceremony – A Handbook for Pastors and Ministers"

Robert Thibodeau

www.ingramcontent.com/pod-product-compliance
Lightning Source LLC
Chambersburg PA
CBHW022306060426
42446CB00007BA/608